HOLIDAY HISTORY
EASTER

by Kristine Spanier, MLIS

pogo

Ideas for Parents and Teachers

Pogo Books let children practice reading informational text while introducing them to nonfiction features such as headings, labels, sidebars, maps, and diagrams, as well as a table of contents, glossary, and index.

Carefully leveled text with a strong photo match offers early fluent readers the support they need to succeed.

Before Reading

• "Walk" through the book and point out the various nonfiction features. Ask the student what purpose each feature serves.

• Look at the glossary together. Read and discuss the words.

Read the Book

• Have the child read the book independently.

• Invite him or her to list questions that arise from reading.

After Reading

• Discuss the child's questions. Talk about how he or she might find answers to those questions.

• Prompt the child to think more. Ask: Easter is a spring holiday. Can you name other holidays that are in spring? Who or what do they celebrate?

Pogo Books are published by Jump!
5357 Penn Avenue South
Minneapolis, MN 55419
www.jumplibrary.com

Copyright © 2024 Jump!
International copyright reserved in all countries.
No part of this book may be reproduced in any form without written permission from the publisher.

Library of Congress Cataloging-in-Publication Data

Names: Spanier, Kristine, author.
Title: Easter / Kristine Spanier, MLIS.
Description: Minneapolis, MN: Jump!, Inc., [2024]
Series: Holiday history | Includes and index.
Audience: Ages 7-10
Identifiers: LCCN 2022043363 (print)
LCCN 2022043364 (ebook)
ISBN 9798885244510 (hardcover)
ISBN 9798885244527 (paperback)
ISBN 9798885244534 (ebook)
Subjects: LCSH: Easter–Juvenile literature.
Classification: LCC GT4935 .S63 2024 (print)
LCC GT4935 (ebook)
DDC 394.2667–dc23/eng/20220922
LC record available at https://lccn.loc.gov/2022043363
LC ebook record available at https://lccn.loc.gov/2022043364

Editor: Jenna Gleisner
Designer: Molly Ballanger

Photo Credits: Shutterstock, cover, 23; 1981 Rustic Studio kan/Shutterstock, 1; New Africa/Shutterstock, 3; Sebastian_Photography/Shutterstock, 4; alefbet/Shutterstock, 5; imageBROKER/Alamy, 6-7; Friedrich Stark/Alamy, 8-9; bilwissedition Ltd. & Co. KG/Alamy, 10; LPETTET/iStock, 11; monkeybusinessimages/iStock, 12-13; JeniFoto/Shutterstock, 14-15; Elena Schweitzer/Shutterstock, 15; NAN728/Shutterstock, 16; Byron Ortiz/Shutterstock, 17; Frippitaun/Shutterstock, 18-19; giulio napolitano/Shutterstock, 19; Visual Cortex/Shutterstock, 20 (left); Irina Fischer/Shutterstock, 20 (right); MesquitaFMS/iStock, 20-21.

Printed in the United States of America at Corporate Graphics in North Mankato, Minnesota.

TABLE OF CONTENTS

CHAPTER 1
Spring Holiday...................................4

CHAPTER 2
Easter Traditions............................10

CHAPTER 3
Easter Around the World................16

QUICK FACTS & TOOLS
Easter Place of Origin....................22
Quick Facts.....................................22
Glossary...23
Index..24
To Learn More................................24

CHAPTER 1

SPRING HOLIDAY

Jesus was born around 6 BCE. He became a religious leader. Many followed his teachings. But some thought he was too powerful. He was **sentenced** to death. He was **crucified** in Jerusalem, Israel.

Jesus

tomb

His body was placed in a **tomb**. The **Bible** says that on the third day, the tomb was empty. Jesus's followers believe he rose from the dead. **Christianity** is based on this. Why? Christians believe there is life after death.

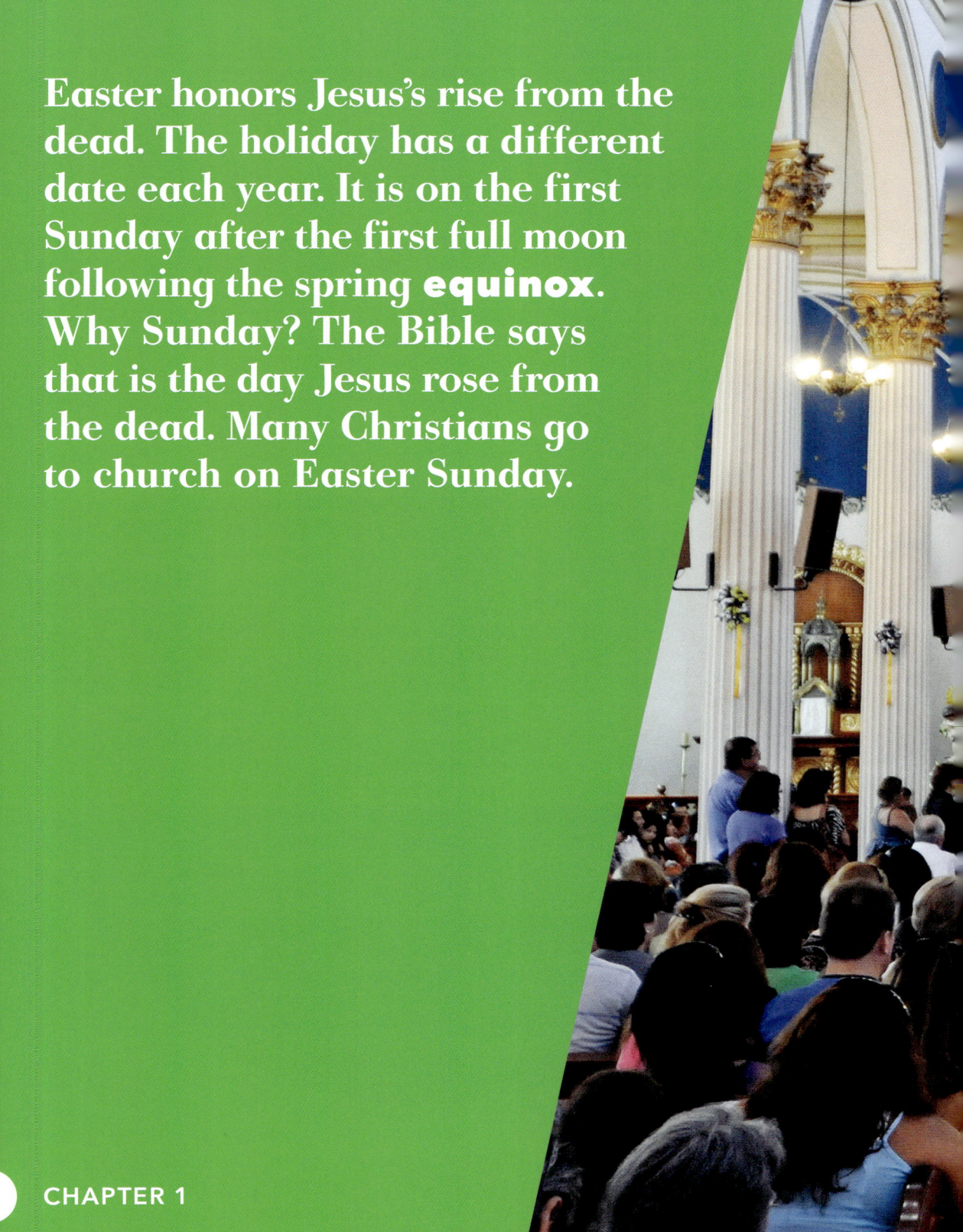

Easter honors Jesus's rise from the dead. The holiday has a different date each year. It is on the first Sunday after the first full moon following the spring **equinox**. Why Sunday? The Bible says that is the day Jesus rose from the dead. Many Christians go to church on Easter Sunday.

CHAPTER 1

Communion

The week before Easter is Holy Week. Holy Thursday honors the final meal Jesus shared with his closest followers. This meal is called the Last Supper. People go to church. They receive **Communion**.

WHAT DO YOU THINK?

The day Jesus died is called Good Friday. Do you think this day should be called something else? Why or why not?

CHAPTER 2

EASTER TRADITIONS

Flowers bloom in spring. Animals are born. Rabbits are everywhere! In the 1600s, Christians in Germany told stories of a hare that brought baskets of eggs to children on Easter. Germans brought this **tradition** to the United States. The hare is now known as the Easter Bunny.

eggs

Lent is the 40-day period before Easter. During Lent, some Christians do not eat certain foods. Eggs used to be one of them. People decorated them instead of eating them. Dyeing and decorating eggs is still a tradition!

CHAPTER 2

CHAPTER 2

On Easter morning, children hunt for hidden eggs. They gather them in baskets. The baskets might have jelly beans, chocolate rabbits, and small toys inside, too.

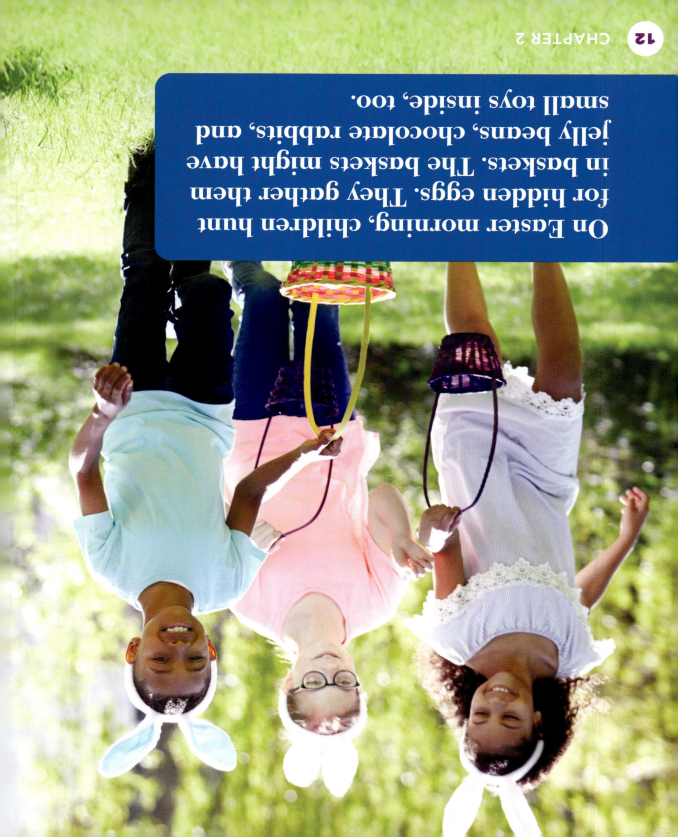

TAKE A LOOK!

What are some **symbols** of Easter? Take a look!

EASTER LILY

BUNNY

EGGS

BASKET

JELLY BEANS

CHOCOLATE BUNNY

CROSS

LAMB

14 CHAPTER 2

People share a special meal on Easter. The meal might include ham, fresh spring vegetables, and egg dishes. There is usually sweet bread, too.

DID YOU KNOW?

A lamb is a popular symbol of Easter. Why? Some Christians call Jesus the Lamb of God.

lamb cake

CHAPTER 2   15

CHAPTER 3

EASTER AROUND THE WORLD

Christians around the world celebrate Easter. People fly kites in Bermuda on Good Friday. Some enjoy hot cross buns. They go to Easter church services on the beach.

hot cross buns

In Guatemala, people make beautiful street carpets. They are made with sand, flowers, fruits, and vegetables. Parades on Good Friday scatter the designs. But that's OK. People make them again the next year!

street carpet

CHAPTER 3

Vatican City

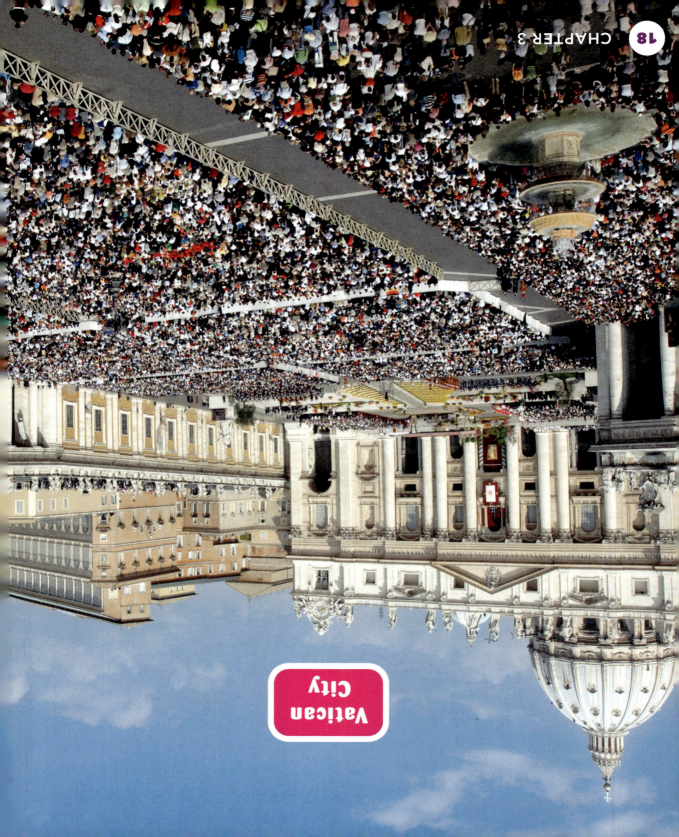

18

CHAPTER 3

Thousands of people go to Vatican City on Easter. Why? They want to hear the pope's Easter message. The pope is the leader of the Catholic Church.

Pope Francis

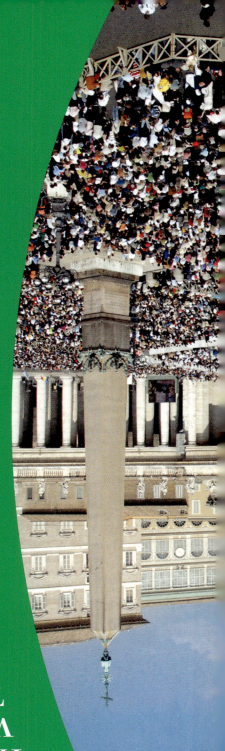

CHAPTER 3

20

Easter is a time for families and friends to gather. It is a time to think about new life. It is even a time to enjoy treats!

WHAT DO YOU THINK?

In Poland, people bring food baskets to church. Priests **bless** the food. Families prepare Easter meals with it. What do you eat on holidays? What makes those foods special?

QUICK FACTS & TOOLS

EASTER PLACE OF ORIGIN

QUICK FACTS

Date: first Sunday after the first full moon following the spring equinox

Year of Origin: around 32 CE

Place of Origin: Jerusalem, Israel

Common Symbols: cross, lamb, bunnies, eggs, baskets, candy, Easter lilies

Foods: ham, lamb, carrots, hot cross buns, chocolate eggs, jelly beans

Traditions: church services, egg decorating, Easter egg hunts, family meals

GLOSSARY

Bible: The sacred book of the Christian religion that contains the Old and New Testaments.

bless: To make holy.

Christianity: The religion based on the teachings of Jesus.

Communion: A Christian practice in which people eat bread and drink wine to remember Jesus's last meal.

crucified: Put to death by nailing or binding the wrists or hands and feet to a cross.

equinox: One of the two days each year when day and night last exactly the same length of time all around the world.

Lent: A 40-day period before Easter during which some Christians remember Jesus, pray, fast, and cut back on luxuries.

sentenced: Officially ordered.

symbols: Objects or designs that stand for, suggest, or represent something else.

tomb: A grave, room, or building that holds a dead body.

tradition: A custom, idea, or belief that is handed down from one generation to the next.

INDEX

baskets 10, 12, 13, 20

Bermuda 16

Bible 5, 6

Catholic Church 19

Christians 5, 6, 10, 11, 15, 16

church 6, 9, 16, 20

Communion 9

Easter Bunny 10, 11

eggs 10, 11, 12, 13, 15

flowers 10, 17

Germany 10

Good Friday 9, 16, 17

Guatemala 17

Holy Week 9

Jerusalem, Israel 4

Jesus 4, 5, 6, 9, 15

lamb 13, 15

Lent 11

meal 9, 15, 20

parades 17

Poland 20

pope 19

symbols 13, 15

tradition 10, 11

United States 10

Vatican City 19

TO LEARN MORE

Finding more information is as easy as 1, 2, 3.

1 Go to www.factsurfer.com

2 Enter "Easter" into the search box.

3 Choose your book to see a list of websites.

FACT SURFER